INCREDIBLE CHANGES ON EARTH

Julie K. Lundgren

A Crabtree Seedlings Book

CRABTREE
Publishing Company
www.crabtreebooks.com

Table of Contents

Water: An Earth System

All the water on a planet forms the **hydrosphere.** Earth's water is found underground, on the surface, and in the air.

System Check
Earth's water may be liquid, solid, or gas.

The hydrosphere

in the air
on the surface
underground

Earth's systems are connected and affect each other. The hydrosphere affects **weather** and **climate**.

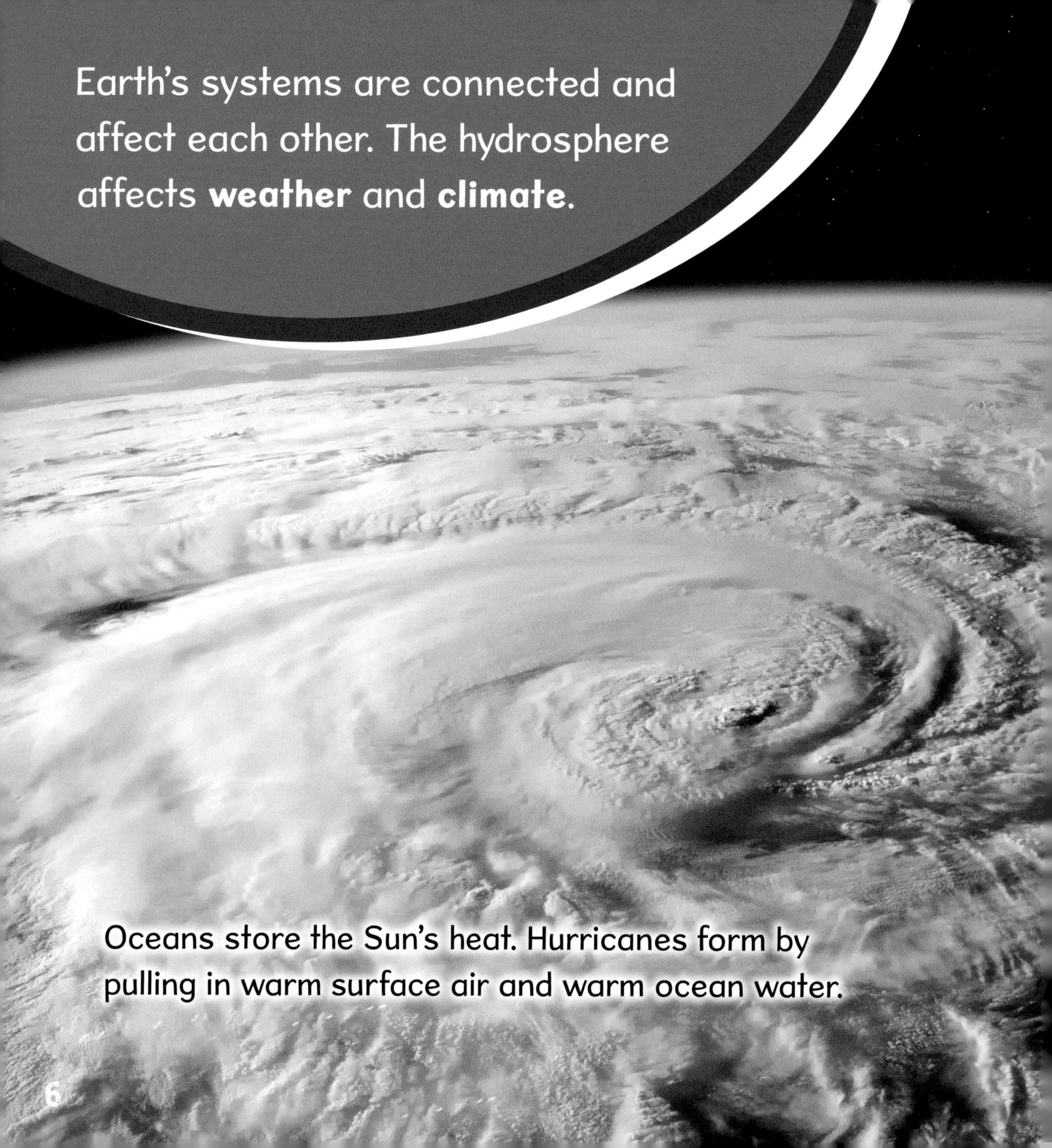

Oceans store the Sun's heat. Hurricanes form by pulling in warm surface air and warm ocean water.

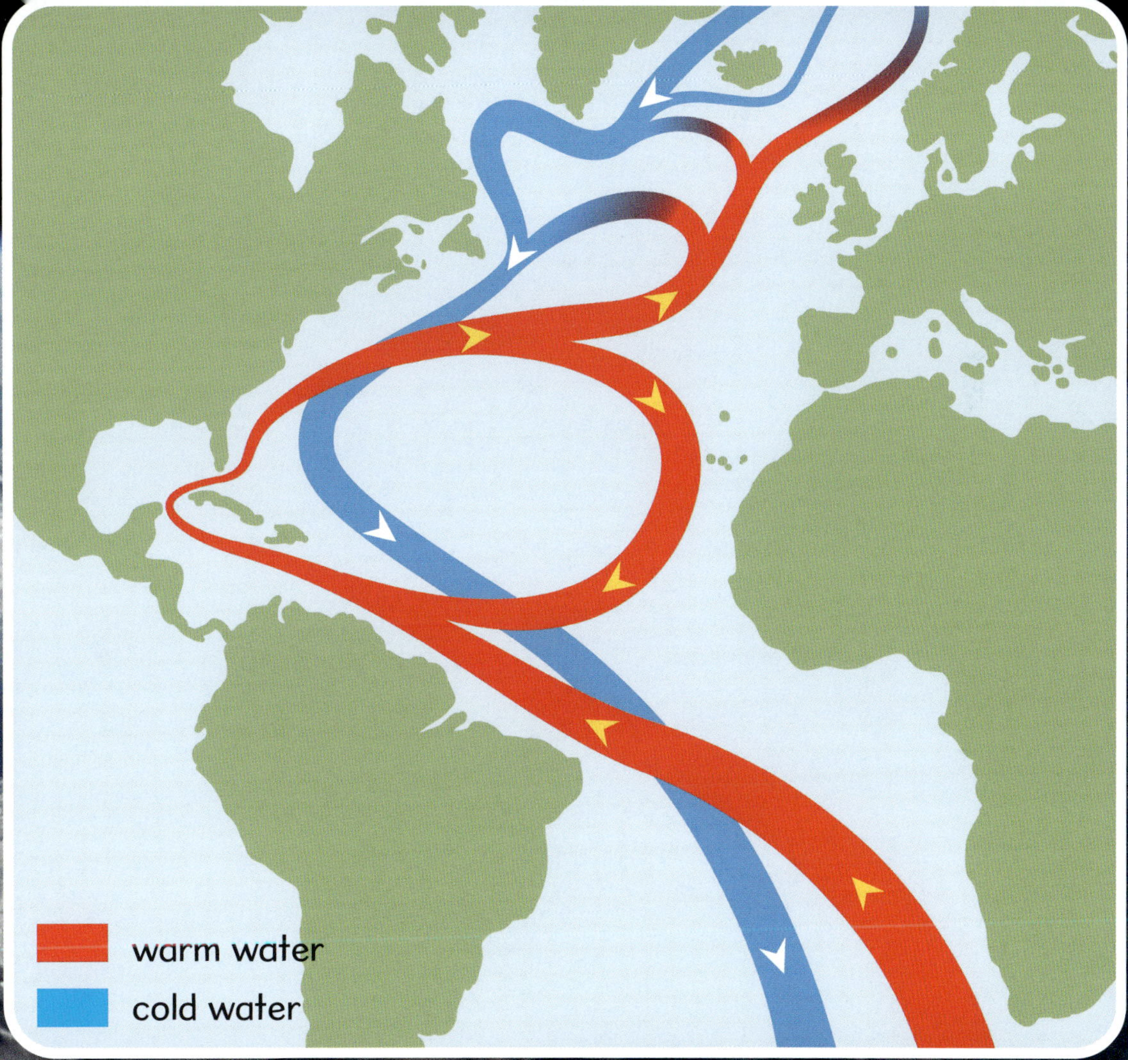

Ocean currents circulate warm and cold water.

The Water Cycle

Water moves in a constant cycle. Liquid water **evaporates** into the atmosphere as a gas. This water vapor returns to the surface as **precipitation**.

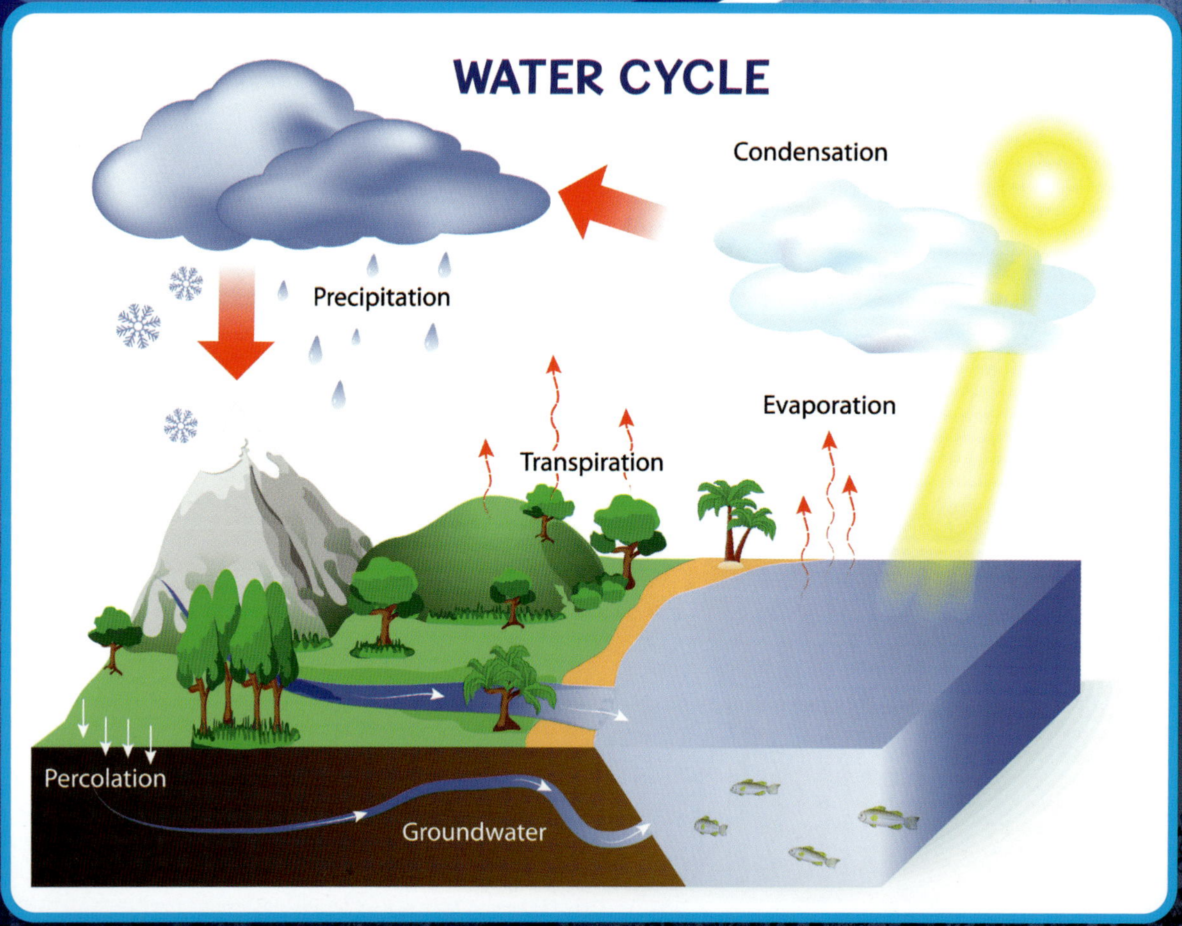

Precipitation includes rain, snow, sleet, fog, and hail.

The Sun, wind, and temperature affect the type and amount of precipitation, and how fast it evaporates.

Warm surface water evaporates. It can form a mist if it reaches cooler air.

Water Habitats

Animals and plants live in freshwater and saltwater. They depend on these **habitats** for shelter and food.

freshwater turtle

System Check
About 71% of Earth's surface is covered in water, and most of that is saltwater.

saltwater fish

Freshwater habitats include lakes, rivers, ponds, and wetlands.

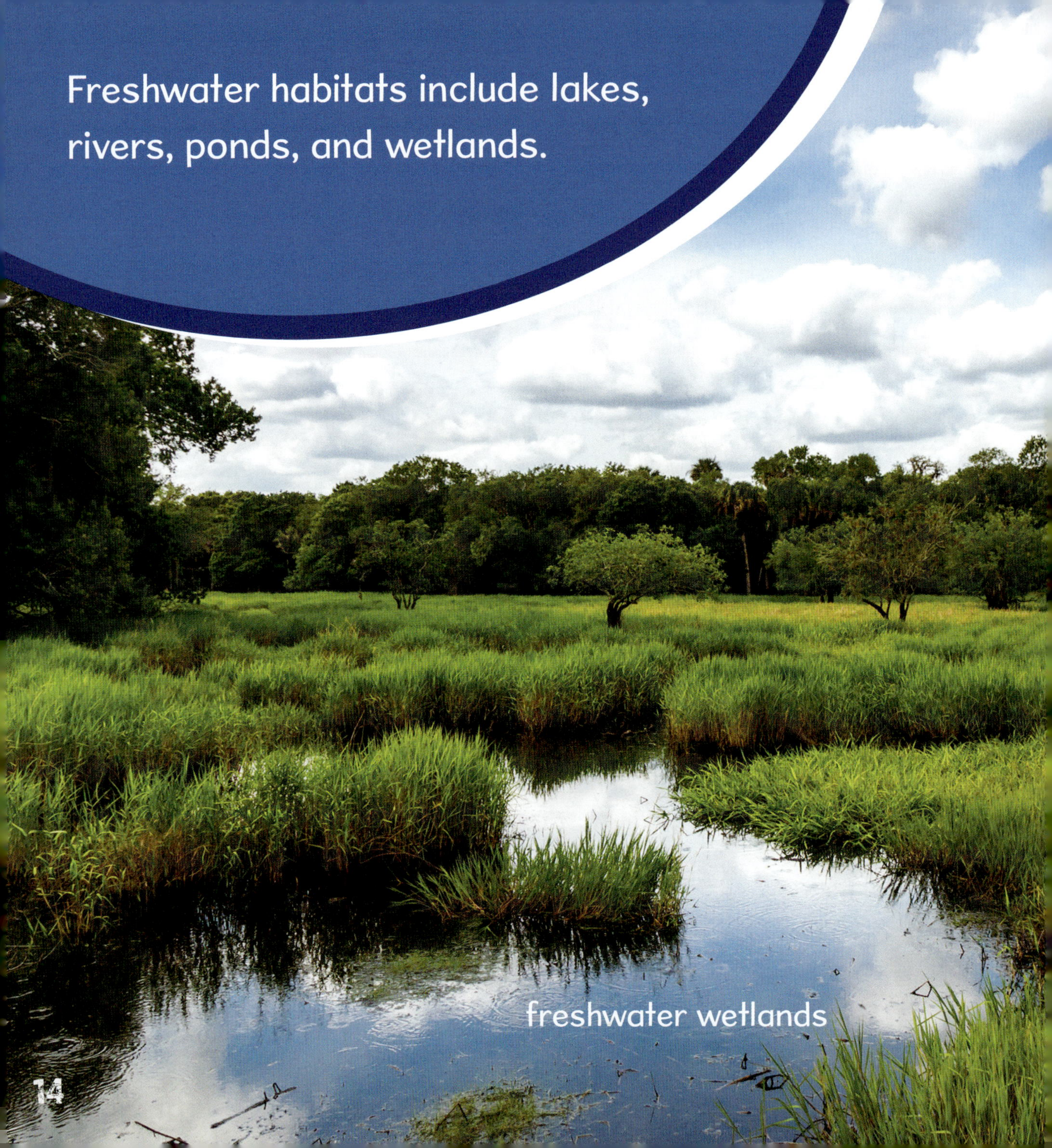

freshwater wetlands

River otters use their sensitive whiskers to help them hunt underwater.

freshwater river

Protect! Don't Pollute!

Our activities endanger Earth's water. Farming, mining, and **manufacturing** may cause water **pollution** and habitat loss.

Salt, fertilizer, and animal waste pollute freshwater habitats.

A huge floating trash zone has formed in the Pacific Ocean.

Climate change causes ocean levels to rise, destroying shores and shallow water habitats. Burning **fossil fuels** adds to climate change.

Burning coal and other fossil fuels for energy pollutes our atmosphere.

Protect our water. Learn about wise water use. How can we meet our needs for energy and food production while keeping Earth clean?

Pick up trash on your next beach visit.

Some people on Earth live without clean water.

Protect water resources. Be a superhero for Earth!

Glossary

climate (KLI-muht): The usual patterns of weather in an area over a long period of time

evaporates (ee-VAP-uh-rayts): Changes from a liquid to a vapor or gas

fossil fuels (FAH-suhl FYU-uhls): Stored energy formed millions of years ago from the remains of plants and animals

habitats (HAB-uh-tats): The natural homes of plants and animals

hydrosphere (HI-druhs-feer): The system that refers to Earth's water, including rain, oceans, rivers, and lakes

manufacturing (man-yuh-FAK-chur-ing): Making products on a large scale, usually in a factory

pollution (puh-LOO-shuhn): Harmful things in the environment, like trash and chemicals

precipitation (pre-sip-uh-TAY-shun): Forms of water that fall from the atmosphere, such as rain, snow, sleet, and hail

weather (WETH-er): The daily wind, sunshine, clouds, and precipitation for an area

Index

WAYS TO PROTECT OUR PLANET

- Learn all you can about climate change.
- Use sand on icy sidewalks instead of salt.
- Pack your lunch in reusable containers instead of plastic bags.
- Turn off the faucet while brushing your teeth.
- Use cloth bags, not plastic.
- Stop using plastic straws.
- Fix leaky faucets and toilets.

We all need clean water!

School-to-Home Support for Caregivers and Teachers

This book helps children grow by letting them practice reading. Here are a few guiding questions to help the reader build his or her comprehension skills. Possible answers appear here in red.

Before Reading

- **What do I think this book is about?** I think this book is about how much water there is on Earth. I think this book is about the power of water and how it helps to change Earth.
- **What do I want to learn about this topic?** I want to learn more about what I can do to protect Earth's water. I want to learn how farming causes water pollution.

During Reading

- **I wonder why...** I wonder why the Sun and the wind affect the amount of rain that falls. I wonder why there is freshwater in lakes, rivers, ponds, and wetlands.
- **What have I learned so far?** I have learned that about 71% of Earth is covered in water, and most of it is saltwater. I have learned that there is huge amount of trash floating in the Pacific Ocean.

After Reading

- **What details did I learn about this topic?** I have learned that precipitation includes not only rain, but also snow, sleet, fog, and hail. I have learned that the Sun, wind, and temperature affect the type and amount of precipitation and how fast it will evaporate.
- **Read the book again and look for the glossary words.** I see the word *hydrosphere* on page 4, and the word *evaporates* on page 8. The other glossary words are found on page 22.

Library and Archives Canada Cataloguing in Publication

CIP available at Library and Archives Canada

Library of Congress Cataloging-in-Publication Data

CIP available at Library of Congress

Crabtree Publishing Company
www.crabtreebooks.com 1–800–387–7650

Print book version produced jointly with Blue Door Education in 2022

Written by: Julie K. Lundgren

Production coordinator and Prepress technician: Tammy McGarr

Print coordinator: Katherine Berti

Printed in the U.S.A./CG20210915/012022

PHOTO CREDITS:
COVER: shutterstock.com| Photobank gallery. Pages 2-3: shutterstock.com | lovelyday12. Pages 4-5: shutterstock.com | Yevhenii Chulovskyi, shutterstock.com | Designua, shutterstock.com | ND700, shutterstock.com|Maria Chapa Hammeken, shutterstock.com | Yevhenii Chulovskyi.. Pages 6-7: shutterstock.com | elRoce, shutterstock.com | Peter Hermes Furian.. Pages 8-9: shutterstock.com | Designua, shutterstock.com | Bill Perry, shutterstock.com | Montypeter.. Pages 10-11: shutterstock.com Tom Wang, shutterstock.com | Matteo Fes, shutterstock.com | AVN Photo Lab. Pages 12-13: shutterstock.com | Shane Gross, shutterstock.com | slowmotiongli, shutterstock.com | katatonia82. Pages: 14-15: shutterstock.com | Irina Mos, shutterstock.com | Ondrej Prosicky, shutterstock.com | TSN52. Pages 16-17: shutterstock.com | Simone Hogan, shutterstock.com | Mr.anaked, shutterstock.com | Fotokostic. Pages 18-19: shutterstock.com | Lux Blue. Pages 20-21: shutterstock.com | Denis Belitsky, shutterstock.com | Yury Birukov, shutterstock.com | David Pereiras. Pages 22-23: shutterstock.com | Davdeka, shutterstock.com | Dave Pot. Back cover: Shutterstock.com | Benjamin M. Weilert

Published in the United States
Crabtree Publishing
347 Fifth Ave.
Suite 1402-145
New York, NY 10016

Published in Canada
Crabtree Publishing
616 Welland Ave.
St. Catharines, Ontario
L2M 5V6